W9-DJP-826

FUN-TO-MAKE

Nature Crafts

Written by Robyn Supraner Illustrated by Renzo Barto

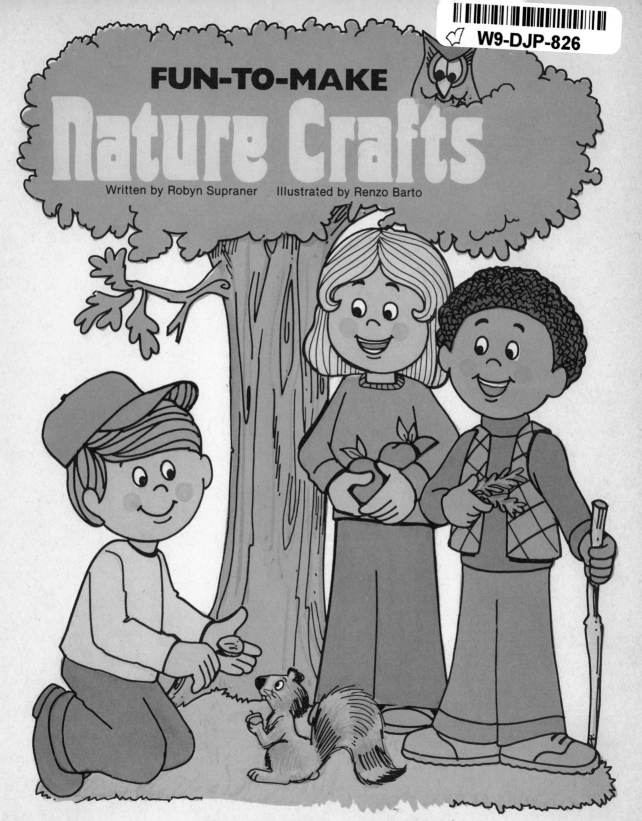

Troll Associates

Library of Congress Cataloging in Publication Data

Supraner, Robyn.
    Fun-to-make nature crafts.

    SUMMARY: Craft ideas using rocks, acorns, nuts,
vegetables, shells, and leaves.
    1. Nature craft—Juvenile literature.
[1. Nature craft. 2. Handicraft] I. Barto,
Renzo. II. Title.
TT160.S92   745.5   80-23999
ISBN 0-89375-440-4
ISBN 0-89375-441-2 (pbk.)

Copyright © 1981 by Troll Associates, Mahwah, New Jersey.
All rights reserved. No part of this book may be used or
reproduced in any manner whatsoever without written permission
from the publisher. Printed in the United States of America.
10 9 8 7 6 5 4 3 2

Autumn is the best time to look for pine
cones, acorns, seed pods, and nuts. Take
along a sandwich (hunting makes you
hungry!) and a bag to hold your treasures.

Use glue and lots of imagination
to put your creations together.

Here are some ideas to get you started!

CONTENTS

ROCKY THE HOUND DOG

Explore a creek bed or the shores of a fast-running stream. Poke around gravel pits or visit a stone quarry. Keep your eyes open—you never can tell. Finding the right rock is half the fun!

Here's what you need:

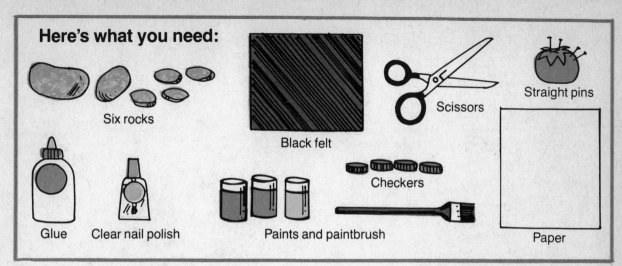

Six rocks

Black felt

Scissors

Straight pins

Glue   Clear nail polish

Paints and paintbrush

Checkers

Paper

Here's what you do:

1   Choose an oval rock for the head. Choose a larger rock for the body. Choose four small rocks for the feet. Make sure these are flat rocks of the same size so Rocky doesn't wobble.

2   Glue the rocks together.

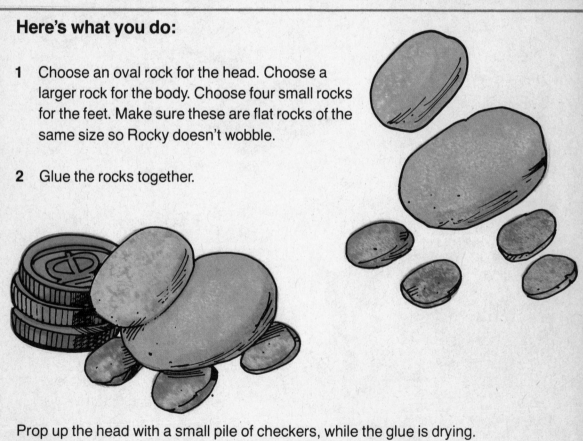

Prop up the head with a small pile of checkers, while the glue is drying. Put Rocky aside to dry for two days or until the glue looks clear.

3 Paint Rocky your favorite color. If you like purple, use it!

4 Paint eyes, a nose, and a mouth. White eyes with black centers look best. Don't forget Rocky's toenails!

5 For a shiny finish, cover Rocky with a coat of clear nail polish.

6 Copy this pattern for Rocky's ears onto a piece of paper.

Cut out the pattern. Pin it to a piece of black felt that has been folded in half.

7 Cut around the pattern, through both layers of felt. This will give you two floppy ears. Cut a bit of felt for the tail.

8 Glue the ears and tail in place.

(*Note*: If you are going to keep Rocky on a table, glue a small piece of felt under each foot. This will protect the table from scratches.)

Here's how Rocky will look when he's done:

Side view

Front view

Top view

For Tommy Turtle:

You can make Tommy Turtle the same way.

1 Choose a small stone for Tommy's head. Glue it to a larger rock. Add the tip of a toothpick for a tail.

2 Paint a fancy design on Tommy's shell. Paint the rest of him green. Add yellow toes. Paint a mouth and two eyes.

For Ladybug:

Use only one rock to make a ladybug. Paint her red. Add white eyes. Use black paint for dots on her body and for the face.

For Bossy Bee:

1   Start with an oval rock. Paint it yellow. Make the eyes black and white. Paint black stripes around the body. Glue part of a toothpick in place for a stinger.

2   Bend a piece of pipe cleaner into the shape of an "8." These are the wings. Glue a piece of tissue paper to the wing shapes. When the glue dries, trim the wings. Bend the wings slightly and glue to the bee's body.

For Pete Penguin:

Side view   Front view

1   Paint all of the penguin and the stand white. When dry, paint the bill and feet orange.

2   Then paint the head and body black.

HANGING CARROT BASKET

Here's what you need:

A big carrot with leaves

Knife

Four pushpins

Four twelve-inch pieces of yarn or string

Here's what you do:

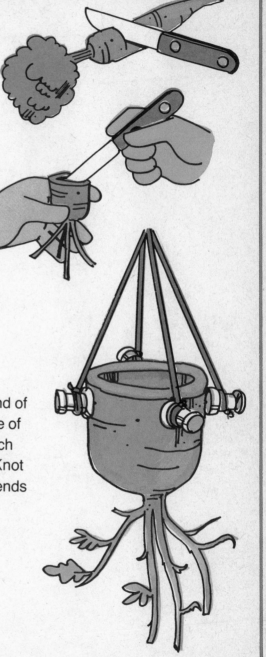

1   With a knife, cut two inches off the top of a big carrot. (*Note*: If you are not allowed to use a knife by yourself, ask a grownup for help.)

2   Strip off the feathery carrot leaves. Do not remove the stems.

3   Carefully, scoop a hollow in the cut end of the carrot.

4   Press four pushpins into the sides of the carrot.

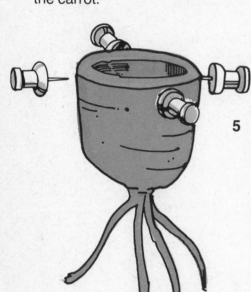

5   Tie one end of each piece of yarn to each pushpin. Knot the other ends together.

6   Hang the carrot from a hook in a sunny window. Keep the hollow filled with water. After a while, new leaves will sprout, and you will have a beautiful plant!

KOOKY CLAY

Here's what you need:

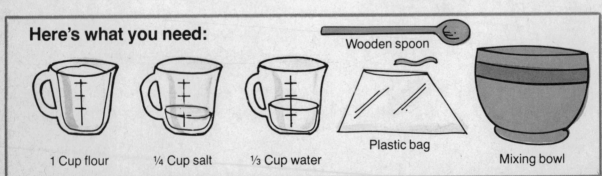

| 1 Cup flour | ¼ Cup salt | ⅓ Cup water | Plastic bag | Wooden spoon | Mixing bowl |

Here's what you do:

1 Put the flour, salt, and water in a bowl.

2 Mix well with a wooden spoon.

3 When the clay is well mixed, press it between your fingers to get out any lumps. (*Note*: If the clay feels dry and crumbly, add a few drops of water. If it feels too mushy, add a bit of flour.)

4 Store the clay in a plastic bag. It will keep for a long time in the refrigerator. Let it warm to room temperature before using it.

Kooky Clay is needed for some of the projects in this book. It is also good for making small figures. It can be painted with any water-base paint. When it is dry, give it a shiny finish by brushing on a coat of clear nail polish.

SNOOPER

This little Snooper has a big nose. All the better to snoop with, my dear!

Here's what you need:

Rolling pin

Paintbrush

Acorn cap

Plastic eyes

Clear nail polish

Wax paper

Peanut

Tiny dried flowers

Seed ball of a sweet-gum tree

Green paint

Kooky Clay

Glass

Glue

Here's what you do:

1 Glue an acorn cap, a peanut, and the seed ball of a sweet-gum tree together, as shown. The stem of the seed ball will be Snooper's tail. (*Note*: Be sure to use enough glue. Some will sink into the holes of the seed ball.)

2 You can buy plastic eyes in a hobby store. Get the kind that jiggle! Glue them in place.

3 On a piece of wax paper, roll out a lump of Kooky Clay. Use a rolling pin.

Cut out a circle by pressing the mouth of a glass into the clay.

4 Stand Snooper on the circle. Press gently until he is standing.

5 Stick a few tiny dried flowers into the Kooky Clay.

6 Wait a few days for the clay to dry. Paint the circle green. If you like, finish it with a coat of clear nail polish.

LITTLE ANNIE ACORN

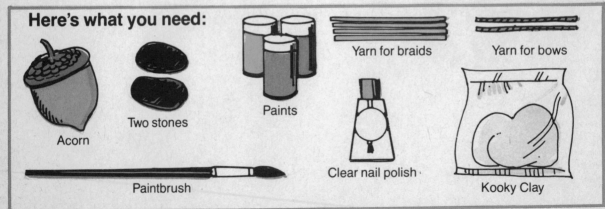

Here's what you need:

Acorn

Two stones

Paints

Yarn for braids

Yarn for bows

Clear nail polish

Paintbrush

Kooky Clay

Here's what you do:

1 With a paintbrush, paint Annie's eyes, nose, and mouth on an acorn.

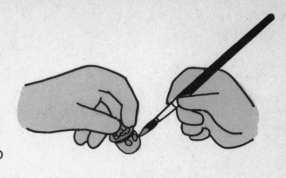

2 Make two braids with colored yarn. Tie them with bows made from yarn of a different color. Glue the braids to the sides of the acorn.

3 Shape Annie's body from Kooky Clay. Set the acorn atop the body. Press it into place. Use two flat, oval stones for Annie's feet. Press the clay body onto the stones. Balance it to make it stand. Set Annie aside to dry for two or three days.

4 Paint a dress on Annie's body. When the paint is dry, brush on a coat of clear nail polish. Polish the acorn, too.

Make Nutty Nellie from a pecan:

1 Tie a triangle of cloth around her head. Use glue to hold it in place.

2 Add two buttons for earrings. Sew the buttons to Nellie's bandana.

3 Paint a happy face!

TOTEM POLE

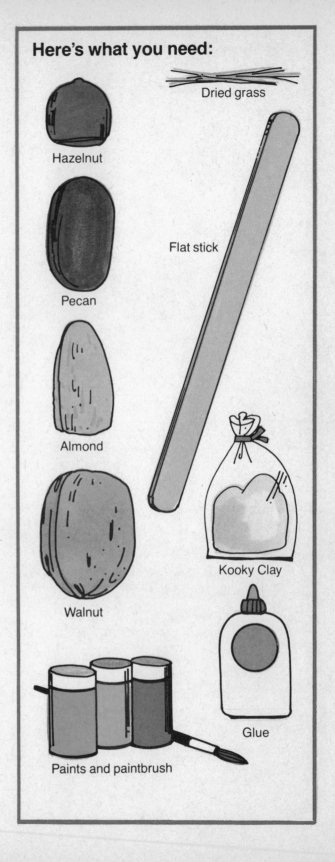

Dried grass

Hazelnut

Pecan

Almond

Flat stick

Walnut

Kooky Clay

Glue

Paints and paintbrush

18

Here's what you do:

1   Paint a face on each nut.

2   Glue the nuts to a stick. Put the walnut on the bottom. Put the hazelnut on top.

(*Note:* Leave a half inch of space at the bottom of the stick to fit into the base.)

Set the stick aside until the glue is completely dry.

3   With Kooky Clay, shape a base to hold up the totem pole. Press the stick into the clay. Press the clay around the stick. Add some dried grass to the base.

4   When the base is dry, paint it brown or olive green. If you like, top off the totem pole with a fancy feather!

(*Note:* Look for feathers in spring and summer. Many lovely feathers can be found along the shore or in the woods. Store them in an envelope.)

TOY RAFT AND BOAT

Here's what you need:

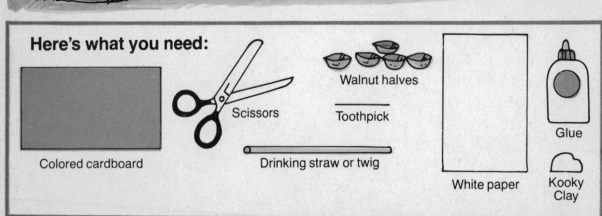

Colored cardboard

Scissors

Walnut halves

Toothpick

Drinking straw or twig

White paper

Glue

Kooky Clay

Here's what you do:

1 To make a raft, glue four walnut shells to a small cardboard rectangle.

2 Cut a sail from a piece of white paper.

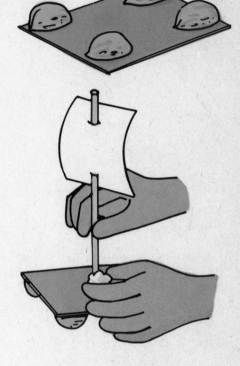

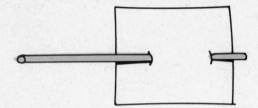

3 Push a drinking straw or a twig through the sail.

4 Attach the straw to the raft with a small lump of Kooky Clay. When the raft is finished, choose a warm, sunny day and merrily, merrily, merrily, merrily float it down a stream!

For a boat:

1 Make a tiny boat from half a walnut shell.

2 Stick a white paper sail on a toothpick. Hold the toothpick in the boat with a bit of Kooky Clay.

FRUIT AND VEGETABLE PRINTS

You can turn a paper bag into something special. Use it to wrap a gift, tote a lunch, or store those greeting cards you have been saving!

GIFT

Here's what you need:

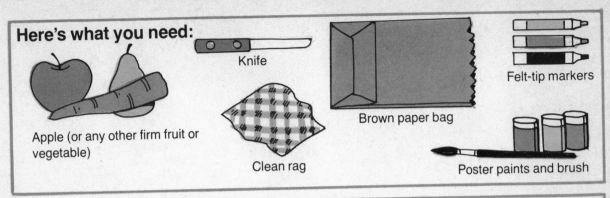

Apple (or any other firm fruit or vegetable)

Knife

Clean rag

Brown paper bag

Felt-tip markers

Poster paints and brush

Here's what you do:

1 Choose an apple with the stem attached. Carefully, cut it in half, lengthwise. Remove the seeds.

2 Pat it dry with a clean rag.

3 Brush a thin layer of poster paint on the cut side of the apple. Choose any color you like. Brush some paint on the stem, too.

4 Carefully, press the painted side of the apple to the paper bag. Lift it gently.

5 Print a row of apples down the side of the bag. Or print a row of apples across the bottom. Or print a circle of apples in the middle. If you like, combine the apple with other fruits or vegetables. Remember to add fresh paint each time you print.

6 With a felt-tip marker, draw tiny seeds in the empty spaces in the center of the apple print.

7 If you like, print "LUNCH" or "GIFT" or "SURPRISE" on the bag.

Can you think of other ways to use fruit and vegetable prints?

SEASHELL PICTURE FRAME

Here's what you need:

Cardboard

Glue

Ruler

Pencil

Ribbon

Nail

Scissors

Clear white shellac and brush

SHELLAC

Picture

Poster paints and brush

Seashells

Here's what you do:

1 To make the front and back of the frame, cut two rectangles of the same size from a sheet of cardboard. Use a pencil and ruler to draw them. *(Note:* Be sure they are at least two inches longer and two inches wider than the picture you are framing.)

2 In the front of the frame, cut an opening for the picture to show through. Cut any shape you like. An oval looks especially nice. With a nail, carefully punch two holes near the top of the rectangle.

3 Choose your favorite color and paint one side of each of the cardboard rectangles. Use enough paint for a smooth, even finish. Wait for it to dry.

4 Decorate the front of the frame with shells. Arrange them to look like flowers or place a pretty border around the opening. Or, if you like, decorate only the corners of the frame. When you have decided upon a design, glue the shells in place. Wait for the glue to dry.

5 To protect the frame, brush on a coat of clear shellac. Brush over and in between the shells. Also coat the back of the frame.

6 Weave a piece of ribbon through the two holes at the top of the front of the frame. Tie the ribbon in a bow.

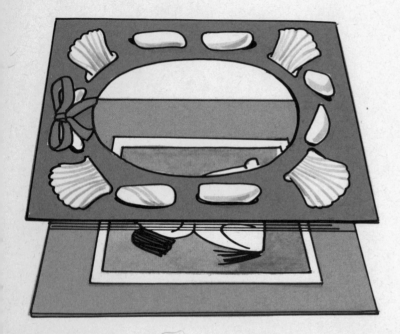

7 Place the picture you are framing between the front and back of the frame. Attach the picture to the back panel of the frame by putting a bit of glue on the back of each of the picture's four corners.

8 Glue the front and back of the frame together. Hold it together until the glue is almost dry.

Here are a few kinds of shells that you may want to use.

To make the stand:

1   Copy the pattern shown to make a stand for a frame that is about 7 inches by 8 inches. (Reduce the pattern for a smaller frame.)

2   Fold along the dotted lines to form the stand. Cut along the solid line. Coat the stand with shellac. Let the shellac dry.

3   Glue the stand to the back of the frame.

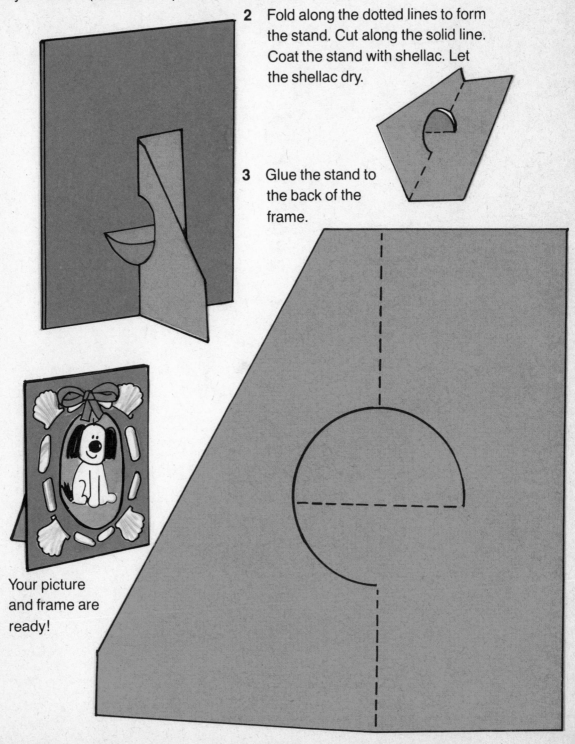

Your picture and frame are ready!

DRIED APPLE GRANNY DOLL

Here's what you need for the doll's head:

Apple

Knife

Vegetable scraper

Kooky Clay

Pencil

Here's what you do:

1 With a vegetable scraper, peel an apple. Use a good size apple. It will shrink as it dries.

2 Carve a face in the apple. (*Note:* If you are not allowed to use a knife by yourself, ask a grownup for help.) Carve large features. They will shrink, too.

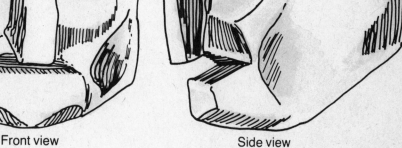

Front view   Side view

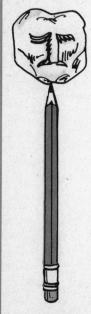

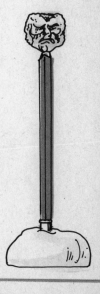

3 Press the eraser end of a pencil into a lump of Kooky Clay. Shape the clay to form a stand. Push the sharpened end of the pencil into the bottom of the apple.

4 Set the apple aside to dry on a sunny window or on top of a radiator.

(Note: The length of time it takes the apple to dry depends on the type and size of the apple. When it looks like a prune, it's ready!)

Here's what you need for the dress:

Cloth for a dress, an apron, and a kerchief

Pink or tan felt

Scissors

Glue

Paper

Pencil

Pins and needles

Thread

Plastic-bag tie

Yarn

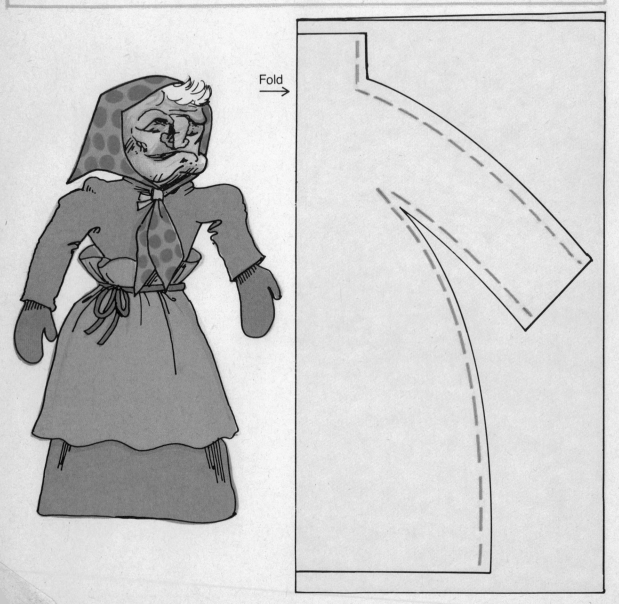

Fold

Here's what you do:

1 On a folded sheet of paper, copy the dress pattern shown on the opposite page. Cut it out.

2 Open the pattern flat and pin it to a folded piece of cloth. Carefully, cut around the pattern. You will have two pieces of cloth that are the same size and shape.

A running stitch

3 Pin the two pieces of cloth together, wrong side out. With a needle and thread, make small running stitches around the sleeves and sides of the dress.

4 Turn the dress right side out.

5 Remove the dried apple head from the pencil. Cover the head with a triangle of cloth. This is her kerchief. Fasten it under her chin with a plastic-bag tie.

6 Place the dress over the pencil and Kooky Clay stand. Replace the head on the pencil.

7 If you like, tie a sash of cloth around her waist with a piece of yarn. This is her apron.

8 You can tuck a bit of cotton under the kerchief. It will look like a wisp of white hair.

9 To complete the doll, you may add hands if you like. Cut small mitten shapes from pink or tan felt. Tuck one hand in each sleeve and sew in place.

TREASURE BOX

Here's what you need:

Paper

Carbon paper

Dry beans

Scissors

Tape

Poster paints and brush

Pencil

Empty cigar box

Piece of felt

Glue

31

Here's what you do:

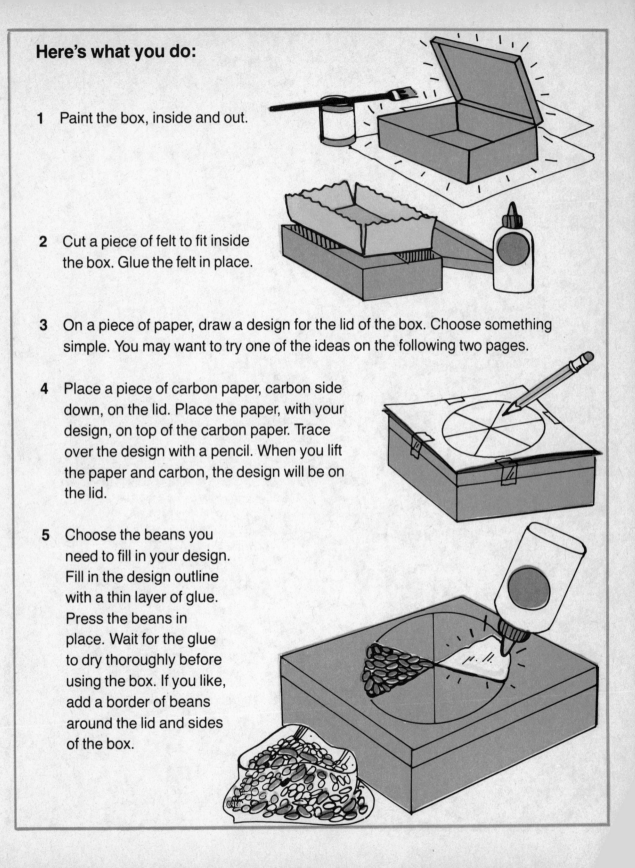

1   Paint the box, inside and out.

2   Cut a piece of felt to fit inside the box. Glue the felt in place.

3   On a piece of paper, draw a design for the lid of the box. Choose something simple. You may want to try one of the ideas on the following two pages.

4   Place a piece of carbon paper, carbon side down, on the lid. Place the paper, with your design, on top of the carbon paper. Trace over the design with a pencil. When you lift the paper and carbon, the design will be on the lid.

5   Choose the beans you need to fill in your design. Fill in the design outline with a thin layer of glue. Press the beans in place. Wait for the glue to dry thoroughly before using the box. If you like, add a border of beans around the lid and sides of the box.

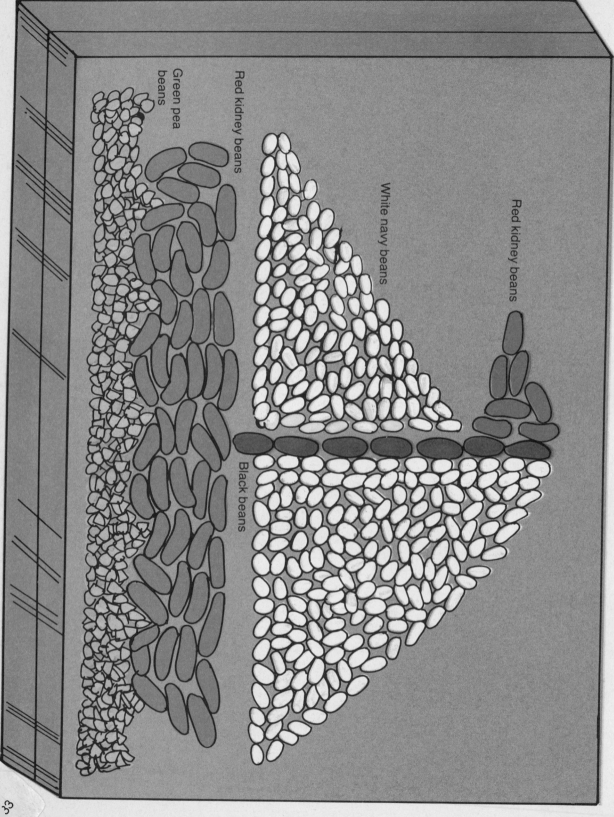

Green pea
beans

Red kidney beans

White navy beans

Black beans

Red kidney beans

33

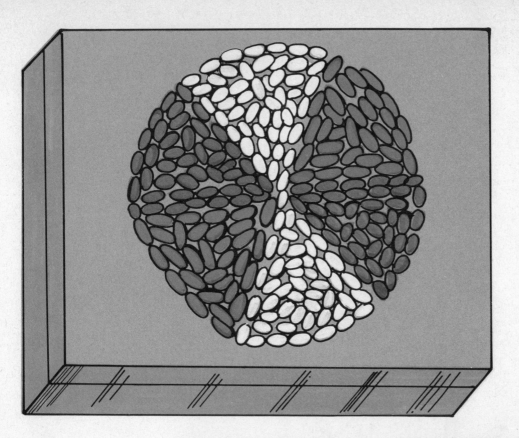

SPATTER PRINTING

Here's what you need:

Red and yellow
poster paints

Old newspapers

Rag

Maple leaf

Oak leaf

Old toothbrush

Clean piece of screening

Smock or old shirt

White paper

Here's what you do:

1 Cover your work space with lots of old newspapers. Wear a smock or an old shirt. Spatter printing is messy!

2 Lay a maple leaf on top of a sheet of paper.

3 Dip an old toothbrush into a jar of red poster paint. Hold a piece of screening over the paper and rub the toothbrush gently across it. Do this until the paper is lightly covered with a spatter design.

4 Carefully, lift up the leaf.

5 Wash the toothbrush and the screen so not a speck of red paint is left. Dry them with a rag.

6 When the first print is dry, place an oak leaf on the paper. Overlapping the shapes will give a nice design.

7 This time, spatter the paper with yellow paint. Lift the oak leaf, and allow the print to dry.

8 Place your print in an old picture frame and give it to someone you like.

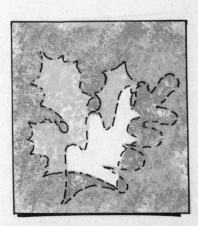

WOODEN SEED PLAQUE

Here's what you need:

Paper towels

Pencil

Wood stain

Sandpaper

Wood scraps

Glue

Nails

Ring from soda can

Toothpick

Hammer

Shellac and brush

Paper

Seeds

Carbon paper

Turpentine

Sponge

Here's what you do:

1   Choose a scrap of wood with an interesting shape. Rub it with sandpaper until it is smooth. Pay special attention to the rough edges!

2   Rub a bit of stain into the wood with an old sponge. Wipe off any extra stain with a paper towel.

3   Punch a hole in the ring from a flip-top can of soda, as shown. Put it aside for a while.

4   On a piece of paper, draw a design to decorate the plaque—a cat, a pineapple, flowers, a butterfly— anything you can think of!

5   Place a piece of carbon paper, carbon side down, on the wood. Place the paper, with your design, on top of the carbon. Trace over the design with a pencil. When you lift the paper, the design will be on the wood.

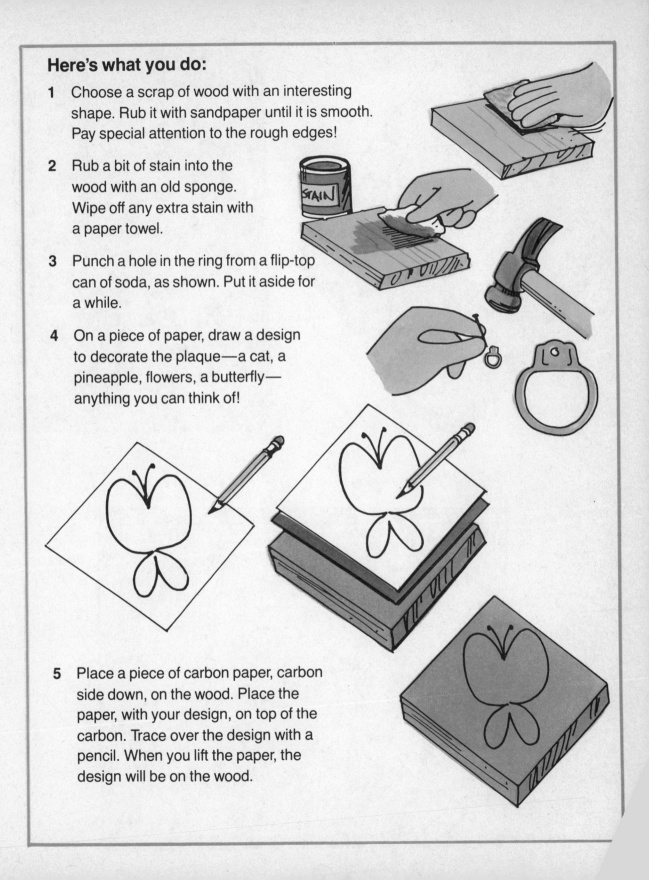

You can use one of these designs or create one of your own.

6 Look at your seeds. Decide where each kind would look best. Melon and pumpkin seeds make good flower petals, eyes, and noses. Yellow popcorn makes perfect buds! Try barley or caraway seeds for a vase or butterfly wings. Look around. You may find some vegetable seeds left over from last spring's planting. Try ruffled pepper seeds to edge a butterfly's wings. Use round radish seeds for black eyes.

Check the spice rack for mustard and poppy seeds. Check the pantry for green and yellow split peas, rice, and groats. Do you have a pet parakeet or canary? Perhaps it has a bit of birdseed to spare!

7 For tiny seeds, spread a thin layer of glue over the space you wish to cover. Then, sprinkle the seeds on the wet glue. Push them into place with a toothpick.

8 Attach larger seeds one at a time. Use a small dot of glue and, carefully, set the seed in place.

9 Wait at least twenty-four hours for the glue to dry. Turn the plaque over, and tap it gently to remove the loose seeds. If there are empty spaces, fill them in.

10 Nail the flip-top ring to the back of the plaque as a picture hook.

11 With a wide soft brush, cover the front of the plaque with a coat of clear shellac. Clean your brush with turpentine.

TERRARIUM

Here's what you need:

Small plants

Knitting needle

Topsoil

Large jar

Wooden spoons

Ground charcoal

Clean sand

Here's what you do:

1 Wash out a large jar and dry it.

2 Pour one inch of sand into the bottom of the jar. Use a wooden spoon to make the sand level.

3 Mix some topsoil with some ground charcoal and pour about one inch of this mixture over the sand. Be careful not to disturb the sand base.

4 Now add about two or three inches of topsoil to form a third layer. Your jar should look something like this. (*Note*: It's best to use sterilized topsoil to keep your terrarium free of insects. You can buy the soil from a garden shop.)

5 When you are at the garden shop, ask the plant dealer to help you pick out the right kinds of plants to use in the terrarium. Or on your next hike in the woods, look for a few small plants to fill your terrarium.

6 Using a wooden spoon, carefully scoop out a small hole in the topsoil. Place a plant in the hole and cover the roots with some soil.

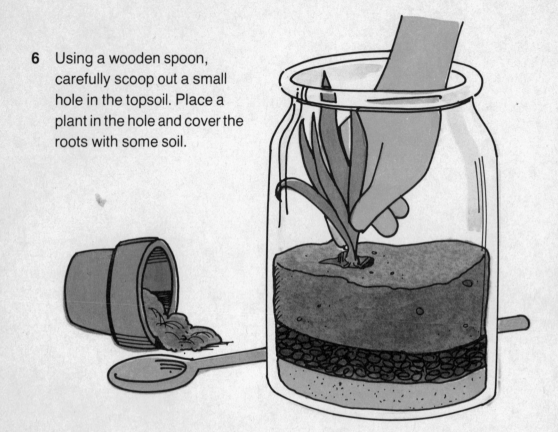

7 After all the plants have been placed inside the jar, add some water to moisten the soil. Do not soak the soil. Terrariums do not need to be watered very often. The water vapor that the plants give off and the water that evaporates from the soil help keep the terrarium moist.

If you want to make a fancier terrarium, you might try this:

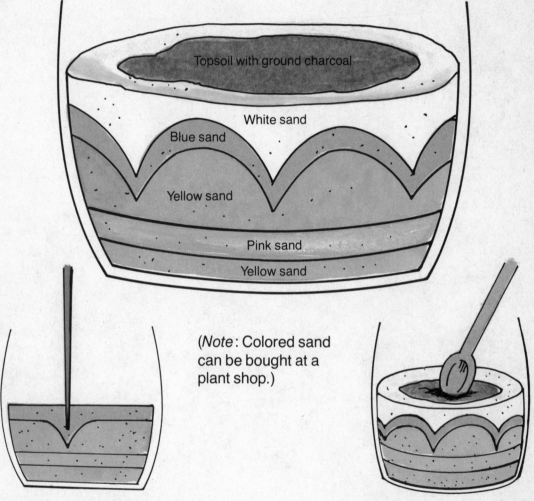

Topsoil with ground charcoal

White sand

Blue sand

Yellow sand

Pink sand

Yellow sand

(*Note*: Colored sand can be bought at a plant shop.)

1 Stick a knitting needle into the yellow sand. Keep it close to the glass, about one-quarter inch above the pink sand. As you remove the needle, pull it toward the center of the container. The blue sand will fill in the space. Do this all around the container.

2 Do the same thing with the white sand. Then, carefully, push the sand to the sides and fill the center with a mixture of topsoil and charcoal. Next place all your plants in the container.

QUICKIES!

Wonder Weed:

If you take the stem of a buck-eye weed and wrap it around and pull it —the little green thing that grows on the end will shoot through the air!

Avocado Pendant:

Wash and dry an avocado seed. Peel off the brown seed coat. With a black marker pen, draw a design on the seed. Glue a piece of yarn to the seed to make a necklace.

Grass Whistle:

Find a broad leaf of grass. Place it between your thumbs. Press your thumbs to your lips. *Blow!*